Jānis Baltvilks

BICKI BUCKI

illustrated by
Reinis Pētersons

A modern nursery rhyme
from Latvia #001

The stone weighs a ton.

Bicki - bucki - boke,

And that's no joke.

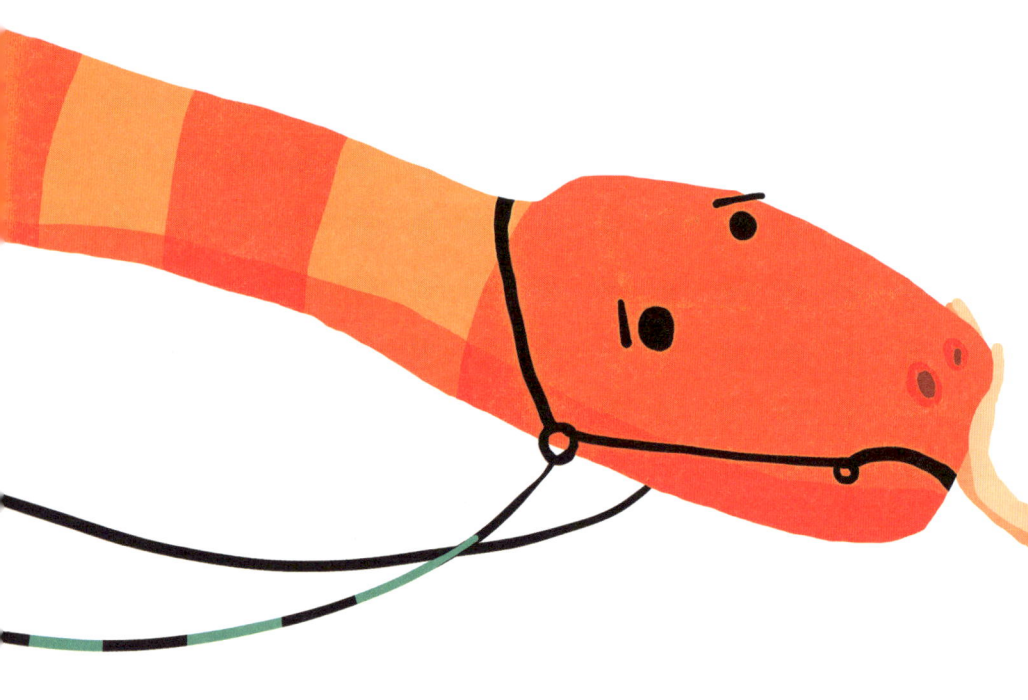

Bicki - bucki - ball,

    My brother's a bit small.

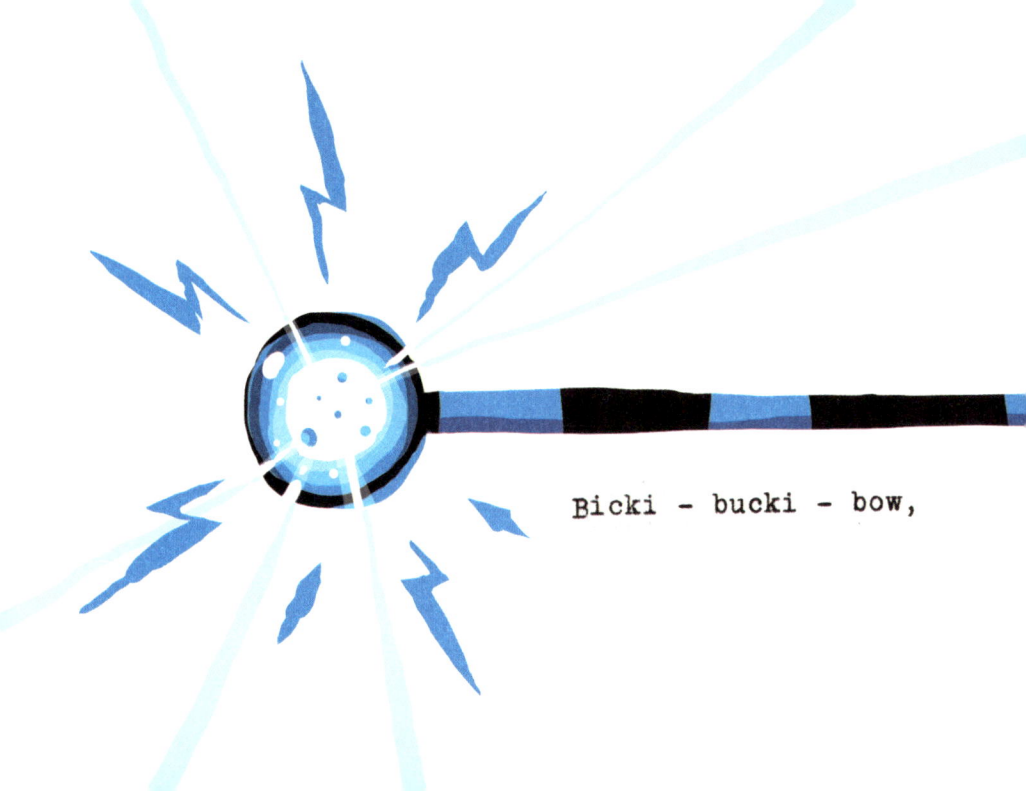

Supported by Latvian Writers' Union (*Latvijas Rakstnieku Savienība*)
and Ministry of Culture of the Republic of Latvia

  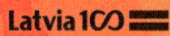

First published in the UK in 2018 by the Emma Press, Birmingham
Originally published in 2012 as "Biki - Buki" by Liels un mazs, Riga, Latvia

Text © Jānis Baltvilks, 1987
English-language translation © Uldis Balodis and Kate Wakeling, 2018
Illustrations © Reinis Pētersons, 2012

BICKI-BOOKS
Artistic director – Rūta Briede
Design – Rūta Briede and Artis Briedis

Printed in Latvia by *Talsu tipogrāfijā*
on *Galerie Art Silk* 170 gsm and *Galerie Art Silk* 250 gsm

A CIP catalogue record of this book is available from the British Library
All rights reserved.

ISBN 978-1-910139-91-2
theemmapress.com